© 2022 Amanda J. Clark. All rights reserved.

No portion of this book may be reproduced in any form without written permission from the publisher or author, except as permitted by U.S. copyright law. For permission contact amanda@disciplingwomen.com.

Published by Divine Appointments Publishing
P.O. Box 41
Allardt, TN 38504

ISBN: 979-8-9875377-1-8

Cover and Illustrations designed by author via Canva.

Visit the author's website at www.disciplingwomen.com

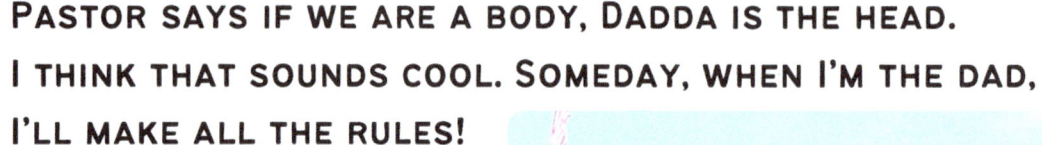

Pastor says if we are a body, Dadda is the head. I think that sounds cool. Someday, when I'm the dad, I'll make all the rules!

If I'm the boss, I won't have to obey. I'll do what I want, and always get my way!

"I will always forgive you.
You are my child.
I must do whatever it takes
for you and God to be reconciled."

What comes next, I don't really enjoy.
His discipline is firm and usually makes me feel sad.
He always reminds me of his love for me
and encourages me to be a good boy.

Dadda says we all need help from a very super power. To take away my sin and help to keep me from doing it again and again.

"I WILL ALWAYS FORGIVE YOU.
YOU ARE MY CHILD.
I MUST DO WHATEVER IT TAKES
FOR YOU AND I TO BE RECONCILED."

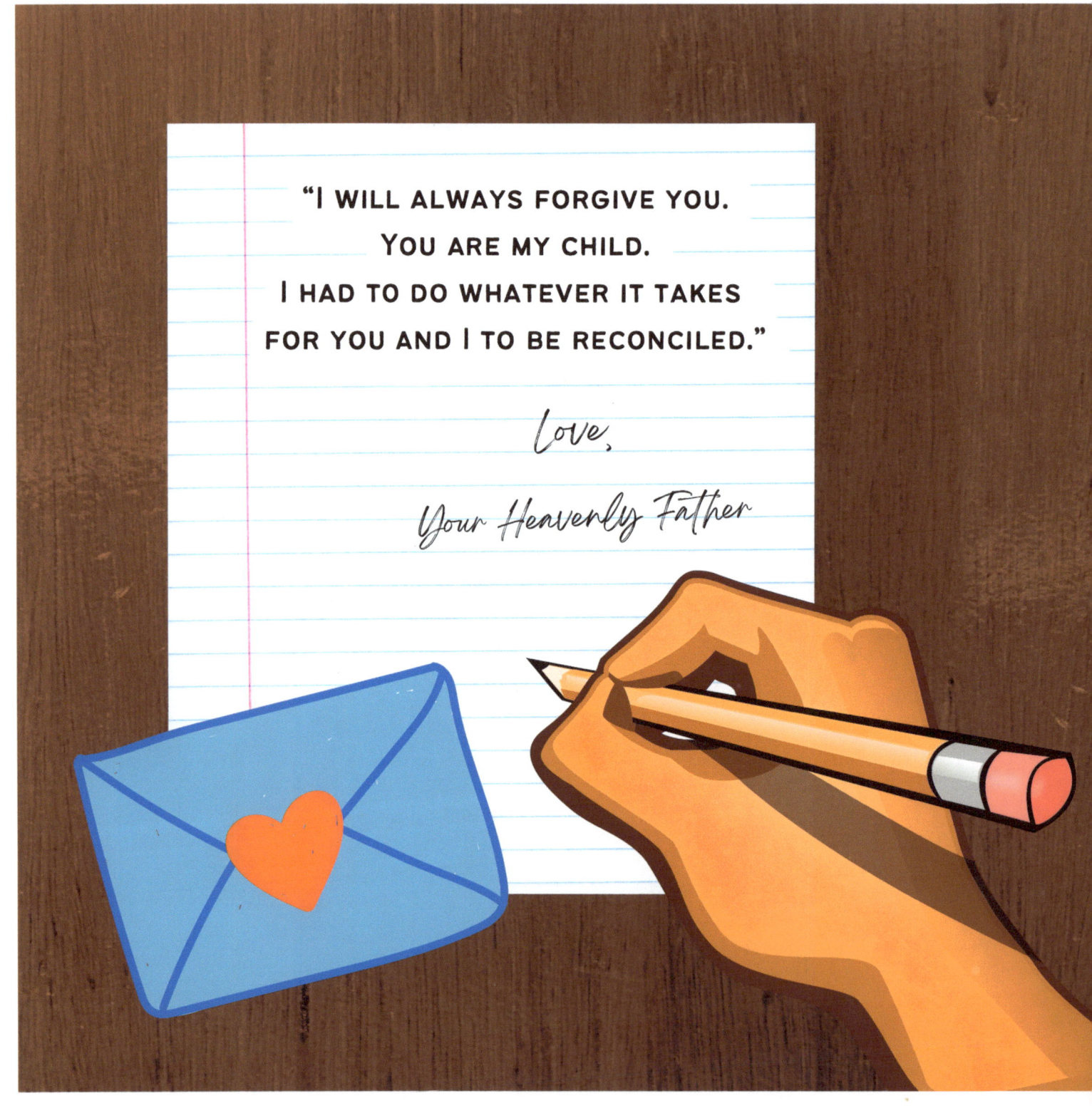

Notes:

- Ephesians 5:22-25
- John 3:16
- Proverbs 3:12 and Proverbs 29
- Hebrews 12:5-22
- Proverbs 19:18
- Romans 8: 37-39
- Ephesians 2
- John 14:1-3

NOTES

God, please help me to remember the ways Dadda loves me like you.

www.disciplingwomen.com